STAR TREK,
anecdotes & curiosities

by Matsuteia

Foreword
BY E.T.A. EGESKOV

Star Trek is one of those mass phenomena that manage to resist the passage of time, to involve different audiences, to unite generations, to resist even their own failures.
And the first television series of the 60s seemed to be destined for failure, the one that gave rise to everything.

Luck, stubbornness, intelligence have allowed its creator and producer, Gene Roddenberry, to make Star Trek much more than an already complex television and film universe but even a possible future experiment, or if you prefer a possible future for humanity.

The coexistence with the other alien races, many of which in fact integrate perfectly with the human one, recalls the cultural and ethnic melting pot that generated the United States of America where Star Trek was born.

And the Federation of Planets looks so much like the Federation of the United States, although probably most Star Trek fans don't even think about it.

The undersigned has a special relationship with Star Trek, because it can boast the privilege, not by merit is understood but only by age, alas, to have seen all the episodes of the original series premiered in Italy, when really that TV series it was futuristic and revolutionary, even for those like me who had seen and appreciated the whole series of Spazio 1999, the British science fiction series aired a few years before Star Trek, at least in Italy.

The advantage of the trekker series was in making the space less distant, perhaps even less fascinating (those who have seen Spazio 1999 know what I'm talking about) but at the same time more accessible, closer, legitimizing science fiction even to those who for science fiction did not try any passion or even abhorred it.

Among the many merits of these television series (films at least for me come in the background) was perhaps having opened the doors of the cosmos to those who perhaps still had their minds too closed on the small kitchen garden.

And if you manage to accept a Vulcans as a hero and a Klingon as a colleague then it becomes difficult to think of words such as racism, discrimination, apartheid.

I remember, incidentally, that when the TV series aired Nelson Mandela was still imprisoned on Robben Island, and racial segregation of apartheid still existed in South Africa!

I like to remember this revolutionary aspect of a television product which, revised today, cannot fail to make people smile (I speak of the original series of the 1960s) for its undoubted flaws.

And even the following series, including films, have not always proved to live up to expectations, but despite this, or perhaps for this reason, they have been able to catch the eye of people and enter the hearts of many people.

Because Star Trek is now a cultural heritage common to all the peoples of this Earth and if it has taught us at least to feel less distant and to be ordinary citizens of this fragile planet then it has far exceeded all expectations of its producer Roddenberry.

Thanks to the authors of this agile booklet that with anecdotes, curiosities and revelations reveal small secrets about the Star Trek saga or remind us of details that perhaps, for those who, like myself, have seen a lot of water pass under the bridges, were lost between trip at warp speed and a jump in hyperspace ... always looking for new forms of life and new civilizations to boldly go where no one has gone before!

*That of Star Trek, enriched over time, has become one
of the most detailed and complex imaginary universes
of all science fiction.*

*It is an optimistic future (albeit after a devastating third
world war) with utopian traits in which humanity has
reached the stars, joining with other species to form a
Federation of united planets and solving all the major
problems that beset the planet Earth (hunger, overpo-
pulation, ethnic discrimination, political divisions and
wars, sources of energy and environmental balance).*

*It is supposed that this could have happened thanks to
the social and cultural stimuli deriving from contact
with extraterrestrial civilizations, more advanced not
only from the technological point of view but, not in-
frequently, also ethically and socially.*

**(excerpt from the page dedicated
to Star Trek on Wikipedia)**

Genesis ... when it all began

Space, the final frontier ... here are the travels of the spaceship Enterprise, during its five-year mission, directed to the exploration of new worlds, to the discovery of other forms of life and new civilizations, up to reaching there, where no man is never come before.

With this sentence began every episode of the famous and unforgettable American science fiction television series conceived by Gene Roddenberry in 1964 and produced since 1966 for the NBC channel and which arrived in Italy only in 1979, the first work from which the whole Star Trek universe was born. then generated other television series, films and literary works.

Filmed on a very limited budget, however, it boasts writers who have become famous (such as Theodore Sturgeon, Richard Matheson and Robert Bloch).

From a social and technological point

of view, the series was decidedly innovative for the times but was not very succes-
sful.

When it made its debut, in fact, neither
the share nor the requests for advertising
spaces were very high.

The second season was even moved
from the first to the second evening (from
20:30 to 22:00) on Friday and rumors
began to spread about a possible cancel-
lation.

She was saved by the few but avid fans,
who organized an unprecedented mobili-
zation so much so that a third season was
granted, at the end of which, however, the
series was interrupted.

The deserved success came with the re-
plicas, only in the following years, which
led to the creation of films and other series, as well as the birth of fan clubs and
the organization of world conventions.

A success that also led to the creation
of a commemorative stamp by the US post
office.

 Matsuteia

In 1976 a veritable avalanche of letters sent by fans to NASA convinced the American Space Agency, to call Enterprise the first Space Shuttle to whose inaugural launch the actors of the series cast were invited in the front row.

THE PILOT EPISODE, OR RATHER NO ... THEY WERE TWO

One of the most well-known curious features of the Star Trek series is the fact that there is a double pilot episode.

Usually when a television series is launched an episode number zero is made (which becomes the famous Pilot episode).

If the audience likes that episode, the series starts, otherwise it cancels in the bud.

The classic Star Trek series was an exception.

The pilot episode was presented in February 1965.

The Cage told the story of the USS Enterprise Federal ship (originally Yorktown) led by Captain Christopher Pike (Jeffrey Hunter) who finds himself grappling with the inhabitants of the planet Talos IV.

Next to Captain Pike appeared a first officer played by Majel Barrett and a Vulcans scientific officer named Spock, played by Leonard Nimoy.

The pilot episode didn't appeal to NBC producers who found it too complex for a series of entertainment, as they intended to do, that didn't force people to think too much.

Some basic ideas, however, seemed promising and, unusually, they decided to offer Gene Roddenberry a second chance.

So the basic story remained almost unchanged, William Shatner was called for the role of Captain James Kirk, but practically the whole cast was changed, except for the character of Spock, who remained in all the series, although deeply transformed.

In the first pilot episode, in fact, the figure of the vulcans presented few differences compared to a human being, mostly of a physical nature (in the first

 Matsuteia

screenplay it had been thought of as a sort of Martian with red skin, in addition to the pointed ears but in it was later decided that the color of the skin should remain normal as, in the still widely used black and white televisions, red appeared black) and the lifting of the eyebrows was added.

In the new pilot episode it was decided to introduce a race in which emotions were completely erased in favor of logic.

Leonard Nimoy was therefore asked to cancel his emotions and to play the double role of First Officer and Scientific Officer aboard the Enterprise.

One of the changes that Gene Roddenberry was forced to make, albeit reluctantly, was that of the figure of a first female officer.

The same women of the time did not seem to appreciate that a woman could command on the ship (in the letters they even wrote sentences like: ... but who do you think you are ...).

Actress Majel Barrett (who will become Mrs. Roddenberry in 1969) was so recycled (once her hair was changed from black to blonde) to play the assistant to the chief medical officer (Dr. McCoy) Cristine Chapel.

Tre sceneggiature erano disponibili per il secondo episodio pilota: When No Man as Gone Before, Mudd's Women and The Omega Glory.

The first of the three was chosen and, a short time after the first pilot episode, the second was presented.

NBC accepted the plan and the series was produced.

Honoring the saying nothing is thrown away, the other two stories available for the second pilot episode then became two other episodes, while the material shot for the first, unfortunate, pilot episode was reused to make the only double episode of the classic series (The mutiny) where the story of Captain Pike is presented as a story that occurred on the Enterprise when this was not yet under the command of Captain Kirk, with a crew previous to that present in the series, the only exception; the presence of Spock who, in some scenes, even sees himself smiling because, as already specified, the figure of the emotionless vulcans had not yet been defined.

CALL ME BY MY NAME,
OR RATHER NO,
DON'T CALL ME AT ALL

During the entire classic series, the first names of Lieutenant Uhura and Sulu were never pronounced.

Of the latter the name Hicaru was made known only in the sixth film The Undiscovered Country.

As for Uhura it was a name that derived from the term Uhuru, in the Swahili language, the title of a text that the actress Nichelle Nichols was reading at the time of being hired for the series.

Uhuru means freedom and the term inspired Gene Roddenberry to play the role of a lieutenant of African descent whose surname was chosen by Nichols herself.

The first name Nyota also comes from Swahili and means star.

Nyota Uhura therefore means Star in freedom.

Make a Vitue of Necessity, the Art of Recycling

When teleportation was invented

The idea of teleportation was born not so much from script needs, as from pecuniary problems.

Considering that every time the members of the Enterprise had to land on a planet or another vessel, there was a need to create special effects (such as landing shuttles, hangars, runways or take-off runways, etc.) all excessively expensive for the budget and even more expensive would have been to hypothesize that the Enterprise could land, since it would have had to be equipped with specific retractable legs (the only ship in the entire Star Trek saga equipped in this sense was the Voyager).

Only in rare cases, in fact, small shuttles have been landed or taken off.

For example, in the episode The Conscience of the King, the model of a shuttle hangar was also used to reduce costs, also used in the following episode The Galileo Seven.

Just for the film The Finale Frontier, Paramount made a real life-size hangar set.

So, to overcome the cost problem, Gene Roddenberry invented teleportation, which allowed crew members to reach ships or planets without any physical movement (and, above all, at low cost).

Darrel Anderson, then, realized the shimmering effect when the teleport was activated by dropping aluminum powder through a light beam and then shooting it all with an upside down camera.

And again for reasons of savings Roddenberry invented the concept of artificial gravity by eliminating the problem of having to create special effects due to the absence of gravity in space.

WE RECYCLE FOR A BETTER WORLD, AH NO! IT'S BECAUSE THERE IS NO MONEY

The limited financial resources available for the realization of the various episodes has characterized the whole history of Star Trek and this explains some peculiarities. For example, most of the federal spaceships are all of the Constitution class, that is, all twins of the Enterprise.

All identical in fact: the Defiant (which disappears in an inter-dimensional space in The Tholian Web), the Constellation (destroyed in The Doomsday Machine), the ships Excalibur, Hood, Lexington and Potemkin (involved in the war simulation against the computer M-5 in The Ultimate Computer) and Exeter (whose crew is transformed into crystals in The Omega Glory).

But also others such as the Nomad spacecraft (in The Changeling) whose structure is partially reused to represent the innovative Romulan concealment system in the episode The Enterprise Incident.

Or like the robot ship first victim of M-5 (The Ultimate Computer) which is the same ship (Botany Bay) where Khan is found in the episode Space Deep (prelude to the second film The Wrath of Khan).

In The Enterprise Incident, Kirk's ship was surrounded by three Romulan ships and, again by virtue of the need to optimize costs, times and resources, the same model as Klingon ships was used instead of making a model of Romulan ship.

During the episode, then, Spock will justify it by saying a simple: the Romulan secret services now use Klingon models. But not only the ship models, the interior has also been the victim of wild recycling. An example? in the episode The Menagerie we see the computer room of Starbase 11 and it is easy to recognize in it the engine room of the Enterprise, while the huge computers are the same used on Eminiar VII for their A Taste of Armageddon.

CHARACTERS, A FIRST LADY, ALIENS, HUMANS AND AN UNPLEASANT KOWN-ALL

THE STAR TREK'S FIRST LADY

Although the classic series is remembered and recognized especially for actors such as Shatner and Nimoy, the faces that represent the Roddenberry saga, there is another character that deserves attention and must be remembered, it is Majel Barrett, first life partner and then wife of Gene Roddenberry.

Nicknamed by fans of the series the First Lady of Star Trek, she could boast the record of having participated in practically all the episodes and several films of the saga.

First in the role of nurse Chapel (who later became a doctor herself), then as Lwaxana Troi, mother of Deanna Troi, both in The Next Generation and in Deep

Space Nine, without forgetting that she voiced the animated series and was the famous female voice of the on-board computer from 1966 to 2005.

After the death of her husband, she continued to work becoming the same producer until her disappearance and subsequent cremation

Her ashes were sent to space as had happened to her husband's.

SNOOTY CAPTAINS

William Shatner, the historic captain Kirk (who does not remember the mythical phrase: Kirk to Enterprise? Repeated in each episode of the original series) was reputed to have a bad character and to be presumptuous, so much so that he even pretended that his name in the titles head was written in a larger font than the names of the other actors.

But his immense ego did not stop at that, he even had other characters cut some lines because by contract he was entitled to a greater percentage of dialogues. Finally, incredible to think of it, but at the beginning he wore shoes with an internal rise to appear taller than colleagues Nimoy and DeForest Kelley (McCoy).

William Shatner had insisted that his contract and Leonard Nimoy's contract contain specific clauses that would prevent both of them from benefiting one another.

These clauses would have served mainly for possible economic negotiations but had less pleasant consequences than Shatner probably would have expected when the saga landed on the big screen.

In fact, Nimoy was hired to direct Star Trek III: The Search for Spock and Star Trek: The Voyage Home (in which he had also contributed to the subject).

Of course Shatner demanded the same treatment and the result was the creation of Star Trek: The Final Frontier, unanimously considered the worst feature film taken from the saga and also despised by most of the protagonists.

Even the script had to be rewritten following complaints from Nimoy and De-Forest Kelley.

1975-1995:
I Am Not Spock – I Am Spock

There was not always a feeling between Spock and Leonard Nimoy, as they say.

On the contrary, there was probably a sort of annoyance on the part of the actor to the idea of being identified (and probably remaining tied) to that role, as demonstrated by the different titles of his two autobiographies, written after twenty years each another, I Am Not Spock (1975) and I Am Spock (1995).

Since in the eighties of the twentieth century the thought of Nimoy was still close to the first title when he was asked to return to play Spock in Star Trek - The Wrath of Khan the actor accepted, placing however a condition: the writing of the film had to include the death of his character.

Which didn't make producers very happy.

They were able to convince him to also shoot an additional scene that could later justify his eventual resurrection (also thanks to the possibility of having Nimoy as director for the third episode), which happened without the participation of the director Nicholas Meyer, who, at the on the contrary, he was convinced that Spock's death should be final.

In a first draft of the script the character should have died almost immediately but, when the fans learned of the plot twist Spock's farewell had to be changed.

The famous greeting vulcans, with the hand raised and the fingers open to V was an invention of the same Leonard Nimoy.

Since he was asked not to laugh and to play an emotionless, as well as extremely logical, character, the actor thought that a handshake or a commonly used gesture would be too warm for a vulcans.

So it was that he thought of a more self-restrained gesture and above all without physical contact.

Or rather, he stole the gesture from a ceremony he had attended at the age of eight in the Synagogue (gesture seen in secret because he should have had his eyes closed), the gesture in fact refers to a Jewish letter which is the initial of Shad-dai , name of God.

Another gesture created by Nimoy, in this case together with Mark Lenard, was that of the touch of the fingers of the Vul-cans, an affectionate gesture for them that was invented specifically for the episode Journey to Babel where the characters of Spock's human mother appear and the Vulcan father Sarek, played precisely by Mark Lenard (who had already played a Romulan officer in the episode "Balance of Terror").

Mark Lenard asked Nimoy to explain the Vulcans psychology to him in order to interpret it better and, considering that the human wife of Sarek would also appear in the episode, Nimoy and Lenard decided that between the two spouses it was possible to think to a gesture of greeting with minimal physical contact (without exaggerating, however, we are always talking about Vulcans)

To highlight the difference between the two versions of the character, Abrams' first feature, the older Spock, played by Nimoy, is mentioned in the credits as Spock Prime, a clear tribute to another series, that of Transformers, at which both the writers Alex Kurtzman and Roberto Orci and Leonard Nimoy himself worked, who lent his voice to the perfidious Galvatron in the 1986 animated film.

Initially, the actor was also considered for the voice of the villain of the same name in Transformers - Revenge of the Fallen (by director Michael Bay, who is also an acquired relative of Nimoy), but had to give up due to other commitments and was replaced by Tony Todd.

He was then engaged, however, later for the part of Sentinel Prime in Transformers 3, a film that also contains several visual and verbal tributes to the character of Spock.

THE JAR JAR BINKS OF STAR TREK OR "SHUT UP, WESLEY!"

It is known that The Next Generation is considered the best series of the saga but we cannot ignore the fact that it contains two annoying elements to say the least.

First it must be said that the first season was made up of episodes that were nothing short of a photocopy of the original series and, secondly, the presence of the character of Wesley Crusher (Wil Wheaton), one of the most unbearable roles that have ever been created, hated by everyone, including the public, so much so that the phrase: Shut up, Wesley! it became a true catchphrase, both in the series and in reality.

Son of Beverly Crusher, young Wesley

arrived on Enterprise D accompanying his widowed mother, who was employed as a medical officer.

The boy was intelligent and Captain Picard, having noticed his potential, immediately integrated him into the crew.

In short, a little genius with great potential but incredibly hateful and know-it-all, until he became one of the most hated characters in the saga audience.

So hated that the same Roddenberry, after a few seasons, resigned himself to cutting it from the series The Next Generation, except to give it a small appearance again a few years later to test any changes in popularity, but without success.

The audience feed back only confirmed the character's high degree of dislike.

The character also won (from Sheldon Cooper in The Big Bang Theory) the somewhat hateful nickname of Jar Jar Binks of Star Trek.

After a while even Wheaton, as much as he loves irony about himself, got tired of it, so much to write on Twitter: From now on I will block everyone who uses that phrase, even if only to joke.

We leave you readers to imagine the answer of his old interstellar travel companion Patrick Stewart ...

CURIOSITIES, MISCELLANEOUS, VARIOUS AND ANY...

The mask worn by the serial killer Michael Myers in John Carpenter's first Halloween movie was actually an official Kirk mask, modeled on Shatner's face and then painted white.

In the name of Captain James T. Kirk, T. stands for Tiberius.

The term Vulcanized, an adjective used in the slang of the official cadets of the Starfleet Academy means: Something made more complex and intricate than necessary (Simple Things Complications Office).

IBM used the word warp internally and then as a final name to identify an OS / 2 release.

Many trekker terms were used within the IBM group of Boca Raton: OS / 2 2.0

was nicknamed Riker, the Geordi Service Pack, OS / 2 2.1 Borg and the whole OS / 2 workplace family (DOS, OS / 2, and AIX) Starfleet. Microsoft was called the Ferengi. In addition to IBM, the name warp has been used by a group of research trekkers from the Carnegie Mellon Department of Robotics for a special computer used in automated vehicle driving experiments.

On the Enterprise ship there are no stairs, only the elevators are used (but in case of failure? Everything stops ...).

In some ducts or pipes of the Enterprise you can notice the writing GNDN; a joke by Dick Brownfield and John Dwyer (respectively special effects curator and set decorator) because the writing means: Goes Nowhere and Does Nothing.

Hikaru Sulu, the helmsman of the Enterprise, was the first intergalactic homosexual character being the clearly gay character, but the thing to be made public had to wait several years.

The female voice of the Enterprise on-board computer both in the classic series and in the The Next Generation series is that of the actress Majel Barrett (the brunette first officer of the first pilot episode and the blonde Cristine Chapel of the series that was later aired).

Terry Farrel (the actress who plays Jadzia Dax), after cutting her lip, asked and obtained that, during the scenes in which she had to kiss Worf (Michael Dorn), the latter could remove the Klingon dentures

The film Frankie and Johnny was shot in a studio close to the one where Star Trek VI was shot, so during the Frankie and Johnny scene where Al Pacino was expected to be surprised after opening a door, the director made sure that Kirk and Spock were behind that door.

In the episode The Cage a green-skinned dancer appears.

Just the green color was the basis of a ... problem worthy of a mystery for Gene Roddenberry.

Since it is common for the colors in the film to not appear as they are seen in reality, Roddenberry made the actress make up and shoot a scene to verify the chromatic result that would be obtained. The next day, shortly after development, the dancer appeared with pink skin.

The test was repeated several times and every time the green color did not appear at all.

The mystery was solved after several tests and the culprit was found who was nothing less than the person in charge of the development, who, not knowing that the dancer should have had green skin, thinking of a defect in the film, had taken care to compensate, being printed, adjusting the skin color from green to pink.

One of the problems encountered by the cast during the filming of the classic series was that of the sliding doors.

As no suitable technology was yet available, the Enterprise doors were manually operated by the crew who had to synchronize with the actors to open and close the doors.

Not wanting to show hesitation when the actors approached the door, which should have been automatic, it often happened that the technicians made the wrong times and they slammed us painfully against the door.

In filmic jargon the red shirts signify those secondary characters, that is, easily expendable.

Have you ever wondered where that saying comes from?

Just from Star Trek, where often the extras who were destined to die during that episode wore the red uniform.

Perhaps not everyone knows that the

Klingon language really exists.

It is a language created by the linguist Marc Okrand starting from the very few lines pronounced by the Klingons in the very first Star Trek film even if, in reality, those words had been invented by Scotty (James Doohan), but they gave Okrand inspiration for the base of the language of the Klingon so that, in retrospect, they ended up making sense.

Patrick Stewart, the British actor who played Captain Picard in Star Trek: The Next Generation was so sure that the series would be a failure that during the first six weeks of filming he even refused to unpack.

The actress Whoopi Goldberg specifically asked to be part of the cast of the TV series because a real Star Trek fan, a request that was initially not taken into consideration since Goldberg at the time was a film diva but in the end she will appear in the recurring role of the bartender Guinan in The Next Generation.

In the opening scene of Star Trek: Generations, Kirk, Scotty and Chekov are invited to pilot the new Enterprise on an inaugural trip.

The journey ends badly with Kirk being sucked into a parallel dimension where he will also meet Picard.

In the intentions, however, originally, the three characters that came from the classic series should have been: Kirk, Spock and McCoy.

However, it had to be changed because DeForest Kelley was ill and did not get insurance to participate in the shooting while Nimoy refused the part, despite being offered the direction of the film.

In the prologue of the Star Trek reboot appears George Kirk, father of James T. Kirk, who sacrifices himself to save his own spaceship attacked by the Romulans. The role was played by Chris Hemsworth and that was his first film appearance before he became a star playing Thor.

Also in the Star Trek reboot to play the role of Spock was called Zachary Quinto who encountered many difficulties in making the Vulcan salute. He struggled to separate his fingers properly and to do this he trained himself by binding his fingers with duct tape.

According to a common opinion of the fans there is a so-called curse of the odd numbers, that is, the Star Trek feature films that had odd numbers have always been considered lower than even ones. Opinion that had to be reviewed with the negative acceptance of Star Trek. Nemesis, the tenth chapter of the film saga (i.e. even) and with the enthusiastic reaction of critics and audiences in the presence of the 2009 reboot which was both the eleventh chapter and the first episode (odd twice).

Ironically, in this new version Simon

Pegg also appears, who in 2001, in his famous sitcom Spaced had stated: In fact, all the odd Star Trek movies suck! then ironic about the sentence during a subsequent interview with the statement: Destiny wanted me to act in that movie to prove that I was shooting bullshit.

The character of Uhura (Nichelle Nichols) was the first colored to appear regularly in a TV series and the kiss that was exchanged with Captain Kirk (William Shatner) was the first interracial kiss in the history of American television.

At the time when the classic series became popular, Leonard Nimoy's father was still working as a barber and often boys were seen entering his shop asking for a haircut like Spock's, totally unaware of the fact that to cut their hair would be he was the real dad of their darling.

In the classic series, originally, for purely practical and economic reasons, the aliens either appeared as a halo of light / energy or almost always appeared in the form of humanoids.

This was also true at the time for the Klingons, the historical antagonists of the heroes of the saga and which continued until the release of the films and television spin-offs. It was then that the look they have to date was adopted, characterized by the famous protruberance on the forehead. It was only during the airing of Enterprise that this aesthetic discrepancy was explained on the grounds that the Klingons seen in the first series were the result of a genetic experiment.

This also gave rise to a nice inside joke: in 1996, in an episode of Deep Space Nine, the protagonists traveled back in time and found themselves on the Enterprise, having noticed the different aspect of the Klingons, the crew asked Worf for an explanation, who replied: Let's not talk about it with strangers!

STAR TREK DID 10

10 EPISODES STAR TREK'S SERIES NEVER MADE

By browsing the internet and doing a search (obviously also making a time jump a bit back in the past) we managed to find some ideas that the different writers, who have alternated in the various generations of the Star Trek saga, have given birth for ten episodes which, thank goodness, have never aired, saving the viewer (perhaps) from the worst science fiction ideas ever made.

So, are you ready for a journey where no man has gone before? and here are the ten tidbit that have never seen the light:

STAR TREK: THE ORIGINAL SERIES
Episode: *Miss Gulliver*

A scientist on board the Enterprise is carrying out experiments on limb regeneration.

Get the situation out of hand, accidentally she begins to grow out of all proportion, creating many problems inside the ship. (But the happy ending could not be missing).

In the finale, her boyfriend also suffers the same fate and both land on a planet where they will give life to a world of giants.

Episode: *The Rebels Unthawed*

The legendary writer Philip José Farmer helped shape Star Trek before the pilot episode was even shot and, later on, proposed some episodes, which Gene Roddenberry found unsuitable.

The third of these episodes never made (however published as short stories by the author), Farmer imagine that the Enterprise discovers a drifting spaceship, in which there are twelve passengers in suspended animation.

The twelve are revealed to be Confederate soldiers who had been kidnapped by aliens during the civil war.

History and cultural shock.

Episode: *He walked among us*

This episode originated from a script by Gene L. Coon and Norman Spinrad, which was rewritten five times before being completely abandoned.

A representative of the fanatic federation of healthy food takes over a planet and declares himself a god.

Being such an action clearly a violation of the first directive, Kirk is forced to intervene, even if dethroning the new king involves throwing the people of the planet into chaos.

Norman Spinrad was so disappointed with the script that he asked Roddenberry to bury him, but in the following years he turned the idea into a five hundred page novel.

Episode: *Bandi*

Kirk is informed that a crew member

has embarked a three-meter-high teddy bear, which however turns out to be an alien

He then orders to destroy it, but he takes pity on him after looking him in the eye and decides to keep him.

Unfortunately all the crew members are plagiarized and end up becoming dominated by the teddy bear, forgetting all their assignments

Kirk, however, discovers the true nature of the object.

In reality, this is an empath who is able to communicate his moods.

Thus, for the second time, he decides to destroy him but becomes the victim of the entire crew who turns against him.

Spock will save the situation, being the Vulcans immune to the effects of Bandi (the giant alien teddy bear).

Moment between horror and absurdity (here we would need the right music but we are not able to write the music, unfortunately, but you can imagine it): after having Bandi locked up, Kirk wakes up in the middle of the night to discover the teddy bear staring at him with evil eyes near his bed.

An episode of the cartoon The Real Ghostbusters also followed this storyline.

Episode: ***Rock a bye baby or die!***

During the Enterprise's visit to a prison planet for mad criminals, the spaceship is possessed by the spirit of a cosmic child who enters the circuits and grows at a dizzying rate (this idea really splits).

In the meantime, Kirk and McCoy must prevent two mad criminals from killing the crocodile men who manage the asylum (but that of crocodile men who manage the asylum splits even more, don't you think?).

Impossible not to list the most embarrassing moments of this script: Uhura who tries to console the spaceship by singing the song that gives the title of the episode.

The cosmic child who directs the ship to the sun (doesn't everyone do it?) Forcing Kirk to electrocute him with a high voltage cable.

The idea of a prison planet for mad criminals run by humanoid crocodiles (we had said that the idea split!).

STAR TREK: NEXT GENERATION

Episode: *Out of time*

While out hunting with Worf, Alexander enters a space-time gap and comes out in a twenty-five year old warrior version (but the idea of a tunnel of eternal youth is beautiful!).

Note that Joe Menoski had proposed the episode for the seventh season as a way to get rid of Alexander, a character he had never liked.

But, according to Renè Echevarria, the idea was not realized because Alexander was the favorite character of Michael Piller's mother.

Episode: *I.Q. test*

By an unknown author but with the collaboration of Herbert J. Wright.

In this script Q would have had an unspecified dispute with another member of the Q continuum, which would have led to a challenge in an arena called Q-olympics between the Enterprise crew and an alien race called Zaa-naar or perhaps the Talarian (there was some confusion about the origins as someone would sing)

Moment of embarrassment (could not miss): one of the stages of the challenge was a game of poker between the two team captains, in which the crew members were living chips (those plastic objects that are used instead of money).

Hey, wait a minute! but somewhere this thing of playing with living pedestrians really does ... but maybe it's chess.

STAR TREK: VOYAGER

Episode: *Q on a beach*

During a Thanksgiving dinner John

Delancie and Brent Spiner proposed an idea, actually just sketched, to Brannon Braga.

L'idea era solo un abbozzo, soprattutto una serie di immagini, con Q su una spiaggia che poteva avere perso la sua identità o la voglia di vivere.

Somehow he was involved in the life of an ordinary person (as could be studied later) and the destiny of this person always in some way (here too the consequences would be studied later) had effects on Q itself

The basic idea became an episode of the fifth season, where an ancestor of Janeaway fell in love with a man who wanted to stop a space project (on the other hand, when ideas are good it would be a shame not to exploit them, what do you say?).

STAR TREK: PHASE II

Episode: *Are unheard memories sweet?*

The crew of the Enterprise is on a journey in search of a missing spaceship, instead finds themselves trapped on a planet dominated by women who are desperate for a man.

Call it bad luck! Some would think but, as they say, not all that glitters is gold and here we are not talking about an episode of pushed science fiction but of an idea that came from a 1882 novel by Walter Besant in which women took control of society but they put aside all scientific research.

The episode would have required many nude scenes, one of the reasons why the network would have refused to air it anyway.

So the episode never materialized, but the idea was still used to make Angel One, considered the worst episode of The Next Generation (on the other hand when it is destined that something doesn't work ...).

STAR TREK: ENTERPRISE

Various ideas on the Porthos dog were

proposed for this series.

Among the ideas never realized: Porthos that develops super intelligence, the presence of an alien dog breed that only it is able to understand and even the dog himself who takes control of the spaceship when the crew is not in a position to do so .

All ideas were rejected (perhaps to prevent the dog from becoming more important than the actors draw attention onto itself).

Star Trek Vs Star Wars

10 reasons because Into Darkness isn't really Star Trek in Trekkers' idea

Always browsing the internet and always doing research we managed to find some information that we thought it necessary to share with you (premising that it is not our opinions but opinions that the trekkers - at least a part of them - has already expressed).

For this paragraph the time jump was shorter and we stopped at a more recent past, precisely landing on the set of "Into Darkness" by J.J. Abrams, director who, as is well known, is more fond of Georges Lucas than Roddenberry's series - of which you can find many curiosities in the previous volume of Matsuteia: Volevo essere uno Jedi – and of which in this film he manages to insert some characteristic elements at the expense of the elements and characteristics that Star Trek have characterized the saga that all trekkers love.

And here are 10 reasons why not all trekkers think Into Darkness is really to be considered part of the Star Trek saga:

Freakshow aliens

If there is one thing that certainly makes you think of Star Wars in the film, it is the representation of aliens.

In Star Trek, aliens have always been extremely anthropomorphic.

A pointy ear, a few speckles on the neck, a slightly curled nose or skin of a different color from humans, sometimes green, sometimes blue.

Choice certainly dictated by limited budgets but also from a conceptual point of view because the Star Trek aliens have always represented others by us, a metaphor for the other terrestrial nations and, from the point of view of the philosophy of Star Trek, they have always put show

how similar others are to us.

In Star Wars, aliens are used to make folklore.

The important characters are more or less almost all human and aliens often seem to be in the race to prove who is more freak

The same happens in Star Trek Into Darkness, where you can see a number of aliens who seem to be circus attractions if not real freaks.

The spaceships

All Star Trek is based on the concept of huge spaceships made to stay in space while the crews teleport (of course the invention of teleportation - as already written previously - was born from economic needs but in fact it is one of the elements that distinguish the saga). In all Star Trek series and films only Voyager, which, it is specified, had special anti-gravity equipment to do so, lands on a planet.

So why in Abrams' film not only does

the Enterprise land, but even go into hiding under water? wouldn't it have remained better hidden if it had remained in orbit?

If you could teleport Spock from the volcano why couldn't you deposit it from the beginning without taking unnecessary risks with the shuttle?

Teleportation becomes super

Already in the first film, teleportation was used from the planet to the spaceship at warp speeds and here we have the villain who presses a button and teleports from Earth to Qo'nos, the main planet of the Klingon Empire.

At this point what are the spaceships for? and what does the other villain do with a super spaceship when he could teleport nuclear bombs to the Galaxy?

Klingon as the clone soldiers of the Empire

After The Next Generation and Deep

Space Nine the Klingons we know them well enough to know that they are proud warriors, they face death in the face and are convinced that being killed in battle is an honor.

With such psychology it is difficult to understand why J.J. Abrams made the Kinglons wear helmets that completely covered their faces, making them look like a squadron of soldiers all the same (as were the clone soldiers of the Empire in Star Wars, in fact).

Carol Marcus, Uhura and the punches

Considering the period in which the classic series was released, it certainly could not be expected that it praised feminism but (as previously written) the female crew members represented decidedly avant-garde female figures for the time.

If we want to compare the Carol Marcus of The Wrath of Khan and that of Into Darkness we have in the first a very valuable scientist, who had an affair with Kirk but left him without regrets or remorse, a strong woman who can take care of herself.

In the second, however, we have a maiden, daughter of a general, who takes advantage of the first opportunity to put on underwear, does practically nothing useful and that in the end (just goes to show) she needs to be saved like any princess who respects.

Uhura herself, who should be an extremely competent officer, in Abrams' film can do nothing but bore the crew and audience with her dissatisfactions in the couple's relationship.

Both have their moment of glory when they impose themselves on Kirk, who would like, as a good macho man, to resolve the situation with a punch, asking to use dialogue instead.

But dialogue does not solve anything.

We are pacifists and inclined to dialogue, therefore far from us, the idea of supporting any form of violence but, perhaps, in the specific case, a good fistfight could also be there).

Pine is Kirk but Kirk will always remain Shatner for everyone

Probably in the common imagination Kirk's image is, has always been and will always remain tied to the features of William Shatner. And Christopher Pine is not Shatner, even if he tries to look like him.

Imitate his gestures, his expressions, even his grimaces.

Not that, in our personal opinion, Shatner has ever had an expression that pierced the screen but Pine really looks like a plastic doll that tries to make imitations.

So better Quinto, who does not look like Nimoy at all and does nothing to do it by giving life to a personal interpretation of his Spock.

What happened to McCoy?

The classic Star Trek series was based

on three main characters: Kirk, Spock and McCoy, almost inseparable.

In Abrams' film there are only two, Kirk and Spock because McCoy is practically absent, he says yes and no a couple of lines throughout the film.

Too much action, few ideas

Pursuits and endless punches .

Is this really what we ask of a Star Trek movie?

We don't really believe.

Star Trek is - like much of the best science fiction - based on ideas and here the ideas are not there, or are old, already seen. Or they are absurd, magical, inappropriate.

Okay, 3D is fascinating, seen at the IMAX then it's the end of the world, but if we wanted a demo on the possibilities of 3D, maybe a documentary about sea turtles was also fine, which in the water have much more sense than the spaceships.

Star Trek is not a place for bad guys

There are many famous villains in the Star Trek saga, but the reality is that - in the series - the point has never been to face villains, but to face problems.

Each opponent in Star Trek had his reasons and the point was not to defeat him, but to find a shared solution.

There are obviously exceptions, especially in the movies.

Especially the last ones, in our opinion, are not enough Star Trek as the two of Abrams.

And of course there is the exception of Khan, in the film The Wrath of Khan.

But in that case there was a well-defined background, there were reasons, there were references to events that happened in the series and there was a plot worthy of the name.

For example, in Into Darkness at some point (you can also see it in the trailer, so it's not much of a spoiler) the Enterprise has to face a bigger and badder Federation spaceship.

If he had been a real Star Trek in that case, the problem would have been the risk of fighting against their colleagues: the crew of the other ship would have had the same uniforms, would have expressed doubts.

Here the problem is exclusively the bad guys, who as such also try to have completely different uniforms and to be made up only of big, big guys and not particularly awake.

Abrams - and his associates Orci, Kurzman and Lindelof - in our opinion the Star Trek series have never seen them, or if they have seen them they have not understood them.

They refer only to films, copying some superficial elements of which they do not understand the reasons.

The quotes, rather than homage, take on the tone of the parody.

Where no one

To do ten, the last element is really geeky: the film ends with the reading of the classic opening phrase, "these are the voyages of the starship Enterprise", is clearly the sentence of the classic series because it refers to "five year mission", but ends with "where no one has gone before".

J.J., "no one" they said it in Next Generation, in the Classic they said no man.

But it's just a detail.

Among the many.

WHEN SCIENCE FICTION IS FUNNY TOO... PARODIES & CO.

Considering that everything, even science fiction, can make people laugh and smile it was inevitable that even the Star Trek universe could have its fair share of irony and produce parodies and more of itself.

We liked to make a small list of these parodies, probably not complete, but certainly curious ...

GALAXY QUEST
by Dean Parisot (1999)

The film is a parody of the science fiction television series, especially Star Trek.

It contains a polite satire of sci-fi fandom, the subculture formed by the community of fans of the series, of which the series is the subject.

The film, in addition to boasting an exceptional cast, including Tim Allen and Sigourney Weaver, has been appreciated among the fans of the genre and critics obtaining several awards: a Silver Screen Award at Amsterdam Fantastic Film Festival, a Silver Ravenal Award at Brussels International Festival of Fantasy Film, a Nebula Award at Science Fiction and Fantasy Writers of America, a Saturn Award all'Academy Science Fiction, Fantasy & Horror Films, an Pegasus Audience Award and a Hugo Award.

And here's the plot in brief: Galaxy Quest is a television series aired between 1978 and 1982 that has generated a following of fans who continue to follow their darlings decades after the suspension of the program.

Unfortunately prisoners of their television roles, the cast members of the series continue in their profession without any passion and, to earn a few extra small change, they wear the role of their characters by inaugurating shopping centers and attending sad conventions for their followers.

Their destinies, however, change when the Termians, strange aliens from the Klatu galaxy, really believe them to be heroes after having seen some episodes of the series.

Thus the aliens come to Earth to kidnap them and convince them to take their side in a war between galaxies.

The actors of Galaxy Request are therefore involved, in spite of themselves, in an alien battle that will lead them to experience on their own skin the dangerous situations that they had only staged for the small screen ... but not everything is really as it appears.

THE ORVILLE
by Seath McFarlane (2018)

The Orville is a parody TV series of Star Trek, where we also find the well-known Charlize Theron in a cameo role in addition to McFarlane himself in the starring role of the series.

McFarlane takes the role of Ed Mercer, a pilot of the USS Orville spacecraft.

After being betrayed and left by his wife, he is offered the opportunity to leave for space, a dream in the drawer that he has always cultivated, an opportunity that he seizes.

Thinking that he can move away from his wrecked life, the pilot cannot imagine finding a surprise that will ruin all his plans.

His ex-wife Kelly Grayson (Adrianne Palickic) is part of the mission as First Officer.

Will the two ex-spouses manage to live together in the confined spaces of a spaceship?

On board, Ed will also find the on-board doctor Claire Finn (Penny Johnson Jerald), the en route officer Gordon Malloy (Scott Grimes) and three aliens: the second officer Bortus (Peter Macon) from the planet Moclan, who does not understand the jokes in spirit, the chief of security Alara Kitan (Halston Sage) and the android Isaac (Mark Jackson), who considers every biological life form (therefore the whole crew) a lower life form and makes no secret of his own opinions , undoubtedly politically incorrect.

The first episode of the series reveals that we are in the 25th century and will immediately enter the heart of the action: the crew will have to save a scientist from a dangerous group of aliens.

STAR WRECK
by Samuli Torssonen (dal 1992)

Star Trek parody film series created by Finnish Samuli Torssonen from 1992.

The first film, Star Wreck, was a simple two-dimensional animation with three starships shooting each other and off-screen voices.

Subsequent films have been improved with more complex and more realistic three-dimensional graphics effects, moreover the duration of each film has been lengthened and the characters, at first simple animations, have been replaced in the last films by real actors

Star Wreck narrates the adventures of James B. Pirk (whose name refers to the character James T. Kirk of the Star Trek series and is played by Samuli Torssonen himself), captain of the starship C.P.P. Potkustart (in English C.P.P. Pedal Start).

The other characters are: Fukov, Spook, Dwarf and Info (inspired respectively by Pavel Chekov, Mr. Spock, Worf, and Data).

All films are shot in Finnish and subtitled in English.

Star Wreck had a loyal group of fans of the sci-fi genre, but it was only after the release of Star Wreck: In the Pirkinning that he was noticed in the international news (downloaded more than 700,000 times during the first week after the release).

Star Wreck: In the Pirkinning it was also broadcast on the Finnish national television YLE and in 2006 it aired in prime time, dubbed in Italian, on the satellite channel Jimmy.

The Star Wreck movies are: Star Wreck (1992), Star Wreck II: The Old Shit (1994), Star Wreck III: Wrath of the Romuclans (1995), Star Wreck IV: The Kilpailu (1996), Star Wreck V: Lost Contact (1997), Star Wreck 4½: Weak Performance (2000) and Star Wreck: In the Pirkinning (2005).

STAR STRIK
(First Episode 1989)

Historic parody based on the famous series where the original films are totally dubbed in the Ferrarese dialect, reassembled and re-edited.

Now become a classic of dementia and trash thanks to the spontaneous diffusion of his videos.

STAR TRASH DEGENERATION
by Fabio Salvati

Episode webseries, parody of the legendary saga directed by a true lover of the original sci-fi series, proof of this is the care with which he used virtual sets and costumes from the classic series.

Star Trash Degeneration is a medium-length film made up of several sketches that makes use of small and functional devices such as laughter and recorded applause typical of sitcoms.

In the first episode you meet the crew of Lentaprise, the intergalactic spaceship that travels in the deepest space, by Captain Krik (Fabio Salvati with a tuft of order and doing set), by Mr. Speck (Michael Jean Backer), by Hurina (Michela D'Organeo), by Mr. Sola (Fabrizio Buzi) and Doctor Rincoy (Tiziano Panetta).

Like any self-respecting parody, even the fiction created and directed by Fabio Salvati, focuses on the most improbable word games and gags that emphasize, mimic and make fun of the characterization of the protagonists of the original series.

START REC.

by Paolo Amadini

Another series of episodes-parody of Star Trek, directed by a fan and made thanks to the participation of 15 non-professional actors.

A real amateur film production, a series of medium length films lasting more than 120 minutes, complete with screenplay, domestic scenography and digital special effects.

The Starship Combat board game, a board game between spaceships, was inspired by Start Rec.

Even the comic classics wanted to be part of the Star Trek universe with *Star Top – Terza Generazione*, Disney saga created by Bruno Enna and designed by Andrea Freccero

Space, the last Gruyere. These are the journeys of the Enter-play spacecraft catapulted beyond the known universe! Where no mouse has ever put its tail.

This is the beginning of the story.

The saga is divided into several episodes and was published in the weekly numbers 3079-3081 and 3162-3165 Topolino (Italian version of Mickey Mouse).

The title refers to the TV series of the 90s Star Trek - The Next Generation, while the characters resume the names of those of the classic series.

On the occasion of the release of the first three episodes of the series during the three weeks of publication of the story plus the following one, a toy gadget was distributed in the annex to the weekly: the USS Enter-Play spacecraft (parody of USS Enterprise) aboard which the commander T.J.J. Tirk (Mickey Mouse) and his crew will explore space beyond the last gruyere, where no mouse has ever put its tail.

In 2016 further episodes were published, always with a gadget attached, dedicated to the series, this time it is the Green Explorer, a model car that runs on solar energy.

And for lovers of racy parodies I found two in particular produced by Revolution X, a manufacturer specializing in classic TV series x-rated remakes (its the x-rated parodies of X-Files and True Blood).

***This ain't Star Trek XXX* e *Star Trek: The Next Geration. A XXX Parody*.** The environments of the Enterprise and the ship itself seem to have been reconstructed with some care, albeit with differences for copyright issues and the crew wears the Starfleet uniforms that we have learned to know also in the cinema films.

The choice of the cast was accurate focusing on actors as similar as possible to the originals (however, for information purposes, not everyone will take off their clothes). For Captain Picard, in the second film, Giles Aston (famous clone of Patrick Stewart) was chosen, whose task will only be to act, maintaining the composure that befits a starship commander.

Ambition, about Star Trek: The Next Geration. A XXX Parody it was not to make a sci-fi x-rated film, but a science fiction film with also pornographic content. Will those of Revolution X have managed to produce an enjoyable story especially for its science fiction aspects, as well as for the carnal ones?

Finally, a short round up of parodies related to one of the characters of the series, who became more famous, could not miss: Spock.

Animaniacs (animated series)
In some episodes Spock makes brief appearances and in the episode Star Truck (parody of the classic series) he is constantly present.

Dr. Slump e Arale (manga and anime)
Spock appears under the name of Skop and its logic is destroyed by the protagonist Arale Norimaki, who alternates mo-

ments of pure presumption with moments of pure madness.

Il laboratorio di Dexter (animated series)

In the series, a friend of Dexter takes Spock's part to go to the Conference of the Galaxies (a meeting of Star Trek fans).

Futurama e ***I Simpson*** by Matt Groening

Leonard Nimoy often dubs himself in the Matt Groening series, where quotations abound referring to the character who made him famous.

Space Last Frontier... Quotes, References, Tributes and a Little Culture...

And in addition to the various parodies already mentioned, a list of references, quotes and tributes that cinema has made precisely to the universe of Star Trek could not be missing.

Boston Legal

by David E. Kelley (2004-2008)

As for references, tributes and quotes to Star Trek I would say that one cannot certainly overlook those that can be intercepted in another TV series, I am talking about Boston Legal, a series halfway between the serious and the facetious aired between 2004 and 2008.

Not only does the cast of the series in question include several well-known faces from the Star Trek series such as

Rene Auberjonois (Odo in Deep Space Nine), Armin Shimerman (Quark in Deep Space Nine e Voyager), Scott Bakula (Jonathan Archer in Enterprise) and, could not miss, William Shatner who together with the histrionic James Spader dominates the action of the serial.

The series contains many self-referential moments and tributes to the universe created by Roddenberry starting from recycled sound effects or the verb cling on, confused with Klingon.

But one of the moments that clearly refers to the series occurs during an exchange of jokes between Shatner and Auberjonois where Shatner says: I am the captain of this ship, you are only a sailor, clear allusion to the difference in rank between Kirk and Odo.

LAND

by Confusion Genesis

Spock's character appears briefly, under the puppet features, in the clip of the 1986 song by the English rock band, in which he is grappling with a Rubik's Cube.

SENTI CHI PARLA

by Amy Heckerling (1989)

Spock's homonymy with the famous pediatrician Dr. Benjamin Spock originated numerous gags in which the two are confused, as in the famous 1989 film, where Mollie (Kirstie Alley) comments on Spock's experience during the Vietnam War and the taxi driver James (John Travolta) replies back with the sentence: Unbelievable! pick on a Vulcan with pointy ears and zero feeling!

Curiously, Kirstie Alley also played the role of the Vulcans Saavik, Spock's best student, in the film Star Trek II - The Wrath of Khan.

Apparently Gene Roddenberry was initially unaware of the pediatrician's existence and only after creating the Vulcans was he informed of the existence of Dr.

Benjamin Spock.

Another Spockian curiosity; the same pediatrician is taken into consideration by Voyager's holographic emergency doctor for the choice of a name to be attributed.

READY PLAYER ONE

by Steven Spielberg (2018)

James Halliday's funeral coffin is a clear reference to Spock's coffin in Star Trek - The Wrath of Khan.

AIRPLAIN II: THE SEQUEL

by Ken Finkleman (1982)

Here William Shatner plays commander Buck Murdock, head of the Alpha Beta lunar base, who, while explore the lunar horizon, sees the iconic USS Enterprise NCC 1701 from his periscope

BLACK MIRROR

by Charlie Brooker (since 2011)

The USS CALLISTER episode of the fourth season of the British series is a tribute to Star Trek.

Director Toby Haynes has revealed other hidden references to the Hollywood Reporter declaring: Michaela (Coel, who plays Shania) she had to be dressed in red because she is the first person to be killed. On Star Trek, in fact, the guy in red is always killed. (Daly is also dressed in red).

Haynes also stated that Jesse Clemons had a vocal coach on set to help him refine his accent, inspired by Captain Kirk played by William Shatner in the original Star Trek series.

We did it once or twice and it looked absolutely Shatner, like when he says Fire at the beginning

Michael Hart, promoter of Project Gutenberg on Internet, he once said: *On some date between today and Star Trek, all that stuff will end up on the computer. Nobody ever questions the fact that all books written throughout human history are on the Enterprise computer, but nobody ever wonders how they got there. We are the ones who put them in it.*

And at this point, after Michael Hart's declaration, we hope that his words are also greetings for this short collection of curiosities, amenities, various and any on the Star Trek universe that more than a book we can define a fun with the which we ventured hoping to send you some curiosity or news of which you were not yet aware and, why not ?, to snatch a few smiles waiting for the next collection.

Matsuteia's note: however I have not given up the dream of being able to lead the Enterprise, I am just waiting for Kirk to retire and leave the job vacant to be able to apply.

ADDENDUM

FILMS

List, not complete, of the main films that make up the saga:

Star Trek (*Star Trek - The Motion Picture*)

Star Trek II (*Star Trek - The Wrath of Khan*)

Star Trek III (*Star Trek III - The Search for Spock*)

Star Trek IV (*Star Trek IV - The Voyage Home*)

Star Trek V (*Star Trek V - The Final Frontier*)

Star Trek VI (*Star Trek VI - The Undiscovered Country*)

Star Trek VII (*Star Trek - Generations*)

Star Trek VIII (*Star Trek - First Contact*)

Star Trek IX (*Star Trek - Insurrection*)

Star Trek X (*Star Trek - Nemesis*)

BOOKS

Several series of novels set in the Star Trek universe have been published, of which about seventy titles have also been translated into Italian.

The events narrated in the novels do not correspond to the canons of the series and are not binding for television series and films.

Some books see the actors of the series as authors (in particular William Shatner).

Four series of novels are original, that is, they are not based on a television series.

Most of the novels are also available as audio books and many of them are read by some of the actors in the series.

In 1967 Bantam Books also published James Blish's fictionalized version of the screenplays of the original series in a series of small volumes, in the same chronological order as the broadcasts.

Since the titles of the novels are very

numerous, I will make a list of them, definitely not complete or exhaustive, inviting readers to do a search on any online platform that deals with selling books where they can spend all the time they want by scrolling through the dozens and dozens of pages where they are listed.

In the meantime, here's a list of the main novel series:

Star Trek – The Original Series
Star Trek – The Next Generation
Star Trek – Deep Space Nine
Star Trek – Voyager
Star Trek – Enterprise
Star Trek – New Frontier
Star Trek – Starfleet Corps of Engineers
Star Trek – Stargazer
Star Trek – Titan

GAMES & CO.

Numerous games and video games have been inspired or derived from the Star Trek saga, as well as role-playing games (which can also be accessed online on specialized platforms), not to mention what we have defined & Co. and which embraces different sectors and types among which one of the most popular is that of gadgets.

Inspired by Star Trek, gadgets of all kinds were created, disseminated and marketed starting from shirts inspired by the fleet uniform, to switch to LED lamps, cups, glasses, puppets, figure actions and many others (mostly objects also available for sale online, if someone has the desire and has the time to take a tour of the stores getting lost in another universe).

The same goes for games and video games.

List all the games born from this universe would become very long so we will just leave a few notes inviting readers to deepen their research (always on the famous online stores or specialized sites).

A game that comes directly from Star Trek is the famous three-dimensional chess game, an ancient game that has achieved some popularity with the classic series.

On the market there are numerous board games inspired by the series, also passing to the construction games (see Lego etc.) or to the figure actions or cards inspired by the characters.

As for role-playing games, they are divided into many types.

They range from live role-playing (usually boardgame) to video games up to online role-playing through forums or chat.

Even for video games, making a list would be impossible, but we believe it is right to mention one that became popular in the seventies of the twentieth century, precisely in 1971, simply titled Star Trek, a textual strategic computer game created by Mike Mayfield and written in Basic language.

Sommario

MATSUTEIA'S BOOKS (ITALIAN EDITION)

are available on Amazon, paperback & ebook

(free on KindleUnlimited)

VOLEVO ESSERE UNO JEDI

with Adele Ross

VOLEVO GUIDARE L'ENTERPRISE
MA KIRK È ARRIVATO PRIMA

with E.T.A. Egeskov

VOLEVO ESSERE UN SUPEREROE
DELLA MARVEL. VOLUME 1

www.ingramcontent.com/pod-product-compliance
Lightning Source LLC
Chambersburg PA
CBHW031144250726

48655CB00002B/833